PASCAL'S WAGER

What Is It To Be Human?

RAY BARFIELD

ISBN: 0615861245
ISBN-13: 978-0615861241

ABOUT THIS SERIES

VeriTalks were created to cultivate ongoing conversations seeded by live Veritas Forum events.

Each VeriTalk includes both the original talk and audience Q&A to draw you more intimately into the conversation. Discussion questions—both personal and intellectual—are incorporated into the talk to deepen your engagement with the material, ideally in the company of friends. The questions are repeated at the end of the book for easy reference.

We hope this series will catalyze your exploration of True Life.

CONTENTS

ACKNOWLEDGMENTS

This talk was originally presented at The Veritas Forum at the University of Oklahoma in 2011 on the sixteenth anniversary of the Oklahoma City bombing under the title, "What Does It Mean to Be Human? Beauty, suffering and being in the world."

Many thanks to the students, faculty and campus organizations who helped create this event.

PASCAL'S WAGER: WHAT IS IT TO BE HUMAN?

WELL, IT'S GREAT TO BE HERE. So what is it to be human? When I heard that you wanted me to speak about this I was humbled, first of all, that you wanted me to speak about anything, and second, that you picked this particular question. After all, what do I know about being human that you don't already know? And it's such a big question. In some ways, the answer is a story about everything.

IMPORTANCE OF THE QUESTION, UNCERTAINTY OF THE ANSWER

So when I got stuck thinking about how to speak about this topic, I did what I usually do and started watching television. And two things came to me. First, as I switched among the various shopping channels, it occurred to me how easy it is to go through life moving from one distraction to the next, never asking the kind of question that you guys are asking tonight. So why this question is important is one fair aspect to address.

The second relevant thing I came across is how tragically common it is to hear on the news that someone either blows themselves up or blows up someone else because they're overly certain that they're right about the human condition. And I'm quite aware about where I'm standing when I say that, and I find it very poignant.

But there's a kind of uncertainty at the heart of human experience that should give us some modest humility as we try to answer questions of such weight, and do so alongside fellow human beings who are also searching, but who disagree with us.

So the importance of the question about what it is to be human and the uncertainty we encounter as we seek an answer, are the two parts of this huge question that I've decided to talk about. Let's tear into it.

Of course, as soon as I start moving towards a response to the question, I realize that I don't know how to answer except as a living person who starts from a particular place. What place is that? I, like everyone, explore from the vantage point of a commitment that's central to my life, work, and thought.

In my case, the starting point is Christianity. This is a commitment that touches on every aspect of the way I view the world. C.S. Lewis said it well when he wrote, "I believe in Christianity as I believe that the sun has risen. Not because I see it, but because by it, I see everything else." But having said that, I have dear friends who are non-theists who deeply disagree with me.

And as I wrestle with my friends who disagree with me but who are trying to get to the truth of things, the truth of what it is to be human every bit as much as I am, I've come to think this is one of the most important forks in the road as we ask our question. What sort of universe are we in? So what I'm giving you today is a snapshot of how I think my way through this question in the midst of uncertainty.

QUESTIONS FOR DISCUSSION

Professor Barfield admits it's easy to move from one distraction to the next, never asking hard questions. So why are you taking the time to dig into the question of being human? What do you hope to gain from dwelling on this question?

PASCAL'S WAGER

To be human is at the very least to struggle towards our end, to struggle in light of our end. Now by 'end,' I mean purpose, but I also mean our death. The question, *Why am I here?* is very nearly a paraphrase of the question, *What is it to be human?* And however the question is phrased, it's profoundly relevant that we ask that question against the backdrop of our mortality. And I suspect that's why you ask me to address this topic.

I teach philosophy in Duke's Divinity School, and at the heart of such teaching are questions such as *Who are we?* and *Why are we here?* But I'm also a pediatric oncologist in the medical school, and so on a daily basis, I take care of children with cancer. There are few things that turn our attention to how short life is and how present death is than working on a pediatric oncology ward, even though I have to tell you it's a very joyful work, and I cure 70% of the kids that come my way.

The ideas that follow are not about death, but they are illuminated by death. I said I'm a Christian, but I don't live my Christian life in absolute certainty, and neither did St. Paul, who embraced faith and hope as proper to this life. Philosophy itself compels me to examine my beliefs using the philosopher's primary tool, which is the question.

So here's a question. What if I do come to an end at my death? Such a question helps me see more clearly what's at stake when we approach this most uncanny of thresholds. Here's another question: What if when I die, I do not come to an end? I either come to an end or I don't. And at first glance, these seem like the kinds of mutually exclusive possibilities that have at least some relevance to how I view the rest of life.

Whatever various writers may say about our posture towards death, whether those writers be Epictetus walking around in his garden or the latest guru in the paperback self-help book section, I'm quite certain for my own journey and from my frequent encounters with the dying of others in my work as a physician, that the questions regarding these two possibilities are experienced with some urgency by many of us.

Indeed, for many, the pain of uncertainty that sometimes looms between the poles of these two possibilities is the fire at the heart of our questioning in between our mysterious arrival and our mysterious departure.

Our questions are about what it is to be human in a world filled with so much beauty and so much suffering. Both beauty and suffering. So as we move deeper into the question of what it is to be human in this world, let's take beauty and suffering as placeholders for the kinds of things we find in the world.

Beauty and suffering exist right alongside one another, and this can leave us reeling. I see it all the time on the oncology ward: a beautiful child suffering from a terrible cancer. And this makes me question the character of the world in which I live. In this uncertain world, I find myself alive, joyful, but full of questions. And not in some trial run, but the only run I have, with each day traded for something, whether I wish to trade it or not.

I'm tiny but am I insignificant? Part of what many people find most annoying about philosophers is that we stand around, staring up at the stars in the night sky and wondering what it all means while the rest of the family is ready to start the movie.

But we can't help it. I can't help it. I look up, and the time it took for starlight to reach my eyes knocks me over. Here again is a question: How is it that I feel myself to mean something important when it took several million light years for the starlight to reach my eyes, only to be extinguished on the cones of my retina, charged to signal starlight to my visual cortex? And why does the light not only yield a brief register of 'starlight,' but also longing and gratefulness and dread all at once in a creature roughly half a century old?

Looking at the stars is an ancient and persistent example of a beauty that can cause this longing for more, even if we can't say exactly what we mean by more. More of what? This longing in the face of stars can even cause suffering in the form of dread, which might be a clue to something important.

Blaise Pascal, the sixteenth-century mathematician and Christian philosopher about whom I'll say more later, would not be surprised to see one of those posters in which the universe is laid out on a map with billions of galaxies shown against a black background, and in red letters, an arrow pointing at a dot that's the Milky Way. The words show up, "You are here." And then there's a box with a picture of our galaxy, and inside that box is another picture of our solar system. And within that one is a picture of the sun, and next to the sun is a dot that shows the relative size of the earth to the sun.

So one obvious conclusion is: I'm tiny. But the question that haunts is: *Am I also insignificant*? Of course, there's no clear reason why a person's size would have anything to do with their meaning. And on this, too, Pascal will have much to say.

Things go much deeper than this, though. When the shock has worn off humanity and a portion of the population retreats to the workplace, another to the four star restaurant, and another to the mall, there's still one often melancholy sort of philosopher who looks around and sees that whatever the sky may seem to say about our tininess, we can still love, we can still care, we can still value, and indeed, we cannot *not* do those things for the most part. And here arises one of the deepest questions of value that binds together all questioning of value in the world.

QUESTIONS FOR DISCUSSION

In the face of the vastness of universe and the complexity of our bodies, people have varied responses. How does the "infinity of universes" affect your thinking about your own significance?

PASCAL'S WAGER

IS IT A CREATED OR NON-CREATED WORLD?

The presence of meaning is something I take to be indisputable, whatever the nature of the universe. But the meaning of meaning, so to speak, depends deeply on what kind of universe we live in. And it's that point that compels me to press on this dividing line between a created versus a non-created universe. This is central to our question of what it means to be a human being, but I do want to underscore before going on that my opinion is that the presence of meaning is itself non-controversial.

And for someone living in an accidental non-created world, how meaning arose is an interesting and important question. But the options that can be entertained to answer that question are clearly different for a person who holds that the universe is created. Both are fascinated by the way in which matter comes to matter to itself as we wake up to the universe.

In a non-created universe, the survival of our species for the brief period that humanity exists means something to me and you, of course, but beyond this, in and of itself, it can have no more meaning than anything else in the universe – some cluster of rocks in another galaxy, the ratio of copper to iron on the planet Neptune, or the black hole nearest our galaxy.

Is love valuable? But even in such a universe, our sense of meaning and value simply *is* as much as any other reality in the universe. For example, whatever account you give of its arrival, love seems to be inherently valuable. Whatever the history of events leading to its existence, whatever material accident or divine will is accepted as a sufficient count of its origin, now that it's here, its value and meaning seem indisputable without of folly or ill-placed reductionism.

Love either emerges from a history of material events, as

does our freedom, our sense of beauty, and our experience of goodness, or it emerges from the character of God, or some combination of these two. In any case, it does emerge and behold, here it is. Now here's a thought experiment to demonstrate the point. Imagine a universe where there's no conscious experience, and therefore, no conscious experience of love. There's nothing but non-living matter expanding, growing colder for the remainder of eternity.

Now imagine the same universe, but in the second universe, two consciousnesses inexplicably emerge and love each other for a single hour before disappearing again. Which of those two universes is more valuable? I'm inclined to say it's the second universe. And if this intuition is right, it suggests that whether love is the very glue of the universe coming from a God who is love, or whether the emergence of love and consciousnesses is merely an accident of a material universe, love is a value. Love is good.

What is the good life? This, of course, is asked from inside our bigger question about what is it to be human. A better way to ask the question might be this: *What is good in human life and why is it good?* Or perhaps: *What is human flourishing?* Before going on, I want to mention again the importance I place on the fact that we don't live in certainty. In a material universe, our lack of certainty is simply a fact. In a created universe, uncertainty may play a role in forming our characters or teaching us to avoid idolatry or any other countless numbers of possible functions.

What are we willing to risk to make sense of the universe? But in our search for what is true about the good human life and the true place of human life in the universe, uncertainty will accompany us throughout, and I take that to be an important part of our experience in being human. In the absence of certainty then, the question is this: What are we willing to risk in order to make sense of the universe? What if there was a strange fact, a fact so strange that it would only be entertained if it was necessary to make sense of the story of experience of the universe as we live it? Well, there are at least two possible facts of this sort.

Two facts, two universes. One of these is that from matter, without life or mind or intention, consciousness grew, and grew to such an extent that it was able to bend back upon itself and become conscious of itself so that at least in this corner of the universe, the universe awakened to itself and began of all things to compose songs of sorrow at the transience of this consciousness, and a universe tending towards destruction.

Another possible explanatory fact is the idea of God as the source of all that we call love, beauty, truth, goodness, and the source of the evolved material flesh we call our brain that's so obviously necessary for our experience of these many goods.

The latter option offers a new kind of exploration, which is an exploration of divine nature. These are two very different universes, both filled with our consciousness of meaning, but with very different perspectives on this meaning. These perspectives shape our projects and our view of what it is to be human.

Now here, the philosophical screw is turned. For life is very short, and I have to choose the projects that will occupy my life against a backdrop about which I can't be certain. Which story is mine? In neither case am I relying on the indubitable nor the irrefutable.

Indeed, in both cases, I'm relying on a kind of faith. But unless my only project is to wrestle with a beast that is the question of which possibility is true, then I must choose. For those who value the weight and the drama of the human dilemma, it's not hubris to choose, and it's not impossible that in so choosing, life itself can deliver up confirmation or disconfirmation.

Meaning of meaning. When I say, then, that I'm a Christian, and a Christian philosopher at that, far from having all questions settled, I'm actually hurled into new questions, plunged into a mystery regarding what it all means. In an uncreated world, there's no real asking about the meaning of the whole, for however much something may mean to me, and genuinely mean in a rich and mature sense, there's no purpose for the whole to have, and mind will soon disappear so there won't be anymore unsatisfied longing for the whole to have purpose.

This is why I say that the nature of the universe seems to me to be a decisive aspect of what it is to be human because it not only determines my place in the universe, but it also determines the meaning of meaning. In my own thinking about what it is to be human, and what it is to seriously question the content of human experience and its meaning, love and beauty are paradigmatic experiences in which we wonder whether there might be more to this universe than meets the eye, including the eye supported and extended by the telescope or the microscope.

PASCAL'S WAGER

QUESTIONS FOR DISCUSSION

Professor Barfield claims that the presence of meaning is indisputable. Do you agree?

What does Professor Barfield mean by "the meaning of meaning"? How does meaning depend on whether you believe the universe is created or not?

Professor Barfield emphasizes the importance of uncertainty in human experience. How does your uncertainty affect your ability to answer hard questions?

? For audience questions related to this topic see page 41 (*If we found an intelligence that values love and truth, would it also be human?*), page 46 (*Is it possible to feel significant, but actually be insignificant?*) and page 51 (*How do you relate meaning and purpose?*).

WHY ARE THINGS THE WAY THEY ARE?

But there's another important part of human experience that dominates the lives of many in this world, and that's the experience of suffering. We suffer, and in our suffering, the same self-aware consciousness that made love and beauty so rich can deepen suffering and thrust upon us an agonizing awareness that things might have been otherwise, forcing urgent questions about why things are as they are. I hear this all the time in my work as an oncologist.

In the experiences of beauty and love, the placeholder for the range of thoughts, feelings, and actions that emerge is gratitude. Is there or is there not someone to thank? With suffering, a question arises, but it's the question whether or not there is someone to blame.

If the universe is not created, suffering is still suffering, but it's not reasonably thought of as inflicted or maliciously permitted, and it provokes no question of why.

But if there's a God responsible for the universe and sufficiently involved to merit prayer, the character of suffering is very different. As they say, now it's personal. Everything that was uniquely and newly attractive about beauty and love in a universe created by God now presses us to ask whether the gains are worth the price.

Framed in this way, the questions that arise tend towards the intractable. They tend towards the intractable not because of a lack of philosophically substantial arguments addressing theodicy. As gratitude for beauty makes no sense without someone to thank, so rage against tsunamis, falling rocks and lightning makes no sense without someone to blame.

But introduce a creator, a sustainer who is a person and not merely some first mover, and suddenly, rage has an infinite target, for the greater the power available to a person to make things otherwise, the greater the fury that they aren't. And yet, rage is by no means a necessary response. It may or may not be the most common response, but it certainly isn't in my experience as a pediatric oncologist. And when it is the response, it's not necessarily a sustained response. This interests me deeply, and it's interested me throughout my career.

Does suffering fit? It also raises a point that underscores the way in which our question about what it is to be human is not some abstraction, but is rather a question that can only be answered from inside of a lived life. Suffering, and our posture towards suffering, perhaps more than any other experience we have, reveals the differences among the possible universes under discussion. Life goes along, and we're quite capable of living without asking a lot of questions.

But when suffering comes, the question whether the universe is created is newly important, bringing a new factor onto the horizon, namely, that of intent to bring about the suffering, or else the willingness to permit it when it might not have been permitted. And rage as a response seems not only understandable, but in the absence of some other way to understand it, it seems almost obligatory. How dare you! I didn't ask for this, but here it is. If it was just pain, I wouldn't like it, but I would tolerate it.

Here's another astonishing human response that arose from inside of a fully lived life: "I am convinced that neither death nor life nor angels nor rulers nor things present nor things to come nor powers nor height nor depth nor anything else in all creation will be able to separate us from the love of God and Christ Jesus our Lord." Or again, "even though our outer nature is wasting away, our inner nature is being renewed, day by day, for this slight momentary affliction is preparing us for an eternal weight of glory beyond all measure because we look not at what can be seen, but at what cannot be seen. For what can be seen is temporary, but what cannot be seen is eternal."

These are both from St. Paul. St. Paul's "slight momentary affliction" included injustice, imprisonment, hunger, whipping, snakebite, shipwreck, and so forth. In this kind of universe, the universe of the apostle Paul, the words "slight" and "momentary" are not a diminutive comment about the suffering inflicted and endured in, say, crucifixion. They do not follow from a worldview that brackets the intensity of our experience of suffering.

I want you to notice this is not theodicy. Theodicy is a philosophical justification of a good God in the face of the fact of evil in the world, and there are many great theodicies available. But what I'm trying to do here is something different. This is an attempt to contemplate the profound enigma of the universe and our experience in it, and to honor this enigma by approaching as a beginner, listening to the tone of experience as it is actually lived.

So sure, set up a horrid scene of suffering, and then with no other information at hand, import an intending God onto the scene and ask the question, "Do these things fit?" And the answer is no.

Love as a starting place. But that's not the universe in which St. Paul lived. The thoroughly created universe is lived not in relation to suffering as a calculus of pain and value, but rather is lived in relation to a loving God. Love is at the starting point.

And with that comes such events in a life as the dark night of the soul, anxiety in the face of suffering, and at the center of the Christian story at least, the words spoken by Jesus from the cross, "My God, my God, why have you forsaken me?" There's no less suffering in such a universe, but the response of lament without grasping for explanation is a response lived every bit as much as the response of gratefulness when beauty erupts to a loving creator.

Corrie ten Boom, who was imprisoned in a Nazi concentration camp, could respond to the circumstances of the Holocaust as she did because of her character, shaped by prior choices and practices of faithful response to God and to others. Her sister, Betsy, was able to say shortly before dying in the Ravensbrük concentration camp, "There's no pit so deep that God's love is not deeper still," because that's the universe in which she and her sister lived. Suffering was perceived and lived in relation to a faithful and loving God rather than God as an abstract concept.

It is in love that we find the heart of the mystery of what it is to be human. Even if love were an illusion, even if all love was finally nothing more than one more version of how chemicals can combine in an accidental, material universe, the consciousness of wanting it to be more than that, the desire for something real beyond the accident of molecular combination, is utterly astonishing and it is at the very heart of the mystery of being human, most evident in our love for another person.

QUESTIONS FOR DISCUSSION

What experiences of suffering have marked your life? How did (or do) those particular experiences fit with your view of the world as created or uncreated?

How is your understanding or response to pain and injustice different if you start with love at the heart of the universe?

Do you think of God more as an abstract concept or a relational being? Can you identify some experiences or people that have shaped this view?

? For an audience question related to this topic (*Do you see patients who are theists handle suffering differently from those who are materialists?*), see page 50.

PASCAL'S WAGER

Two Kinds of Thinkers

So central is this mystery, so compelling is this need, that there's little satisfaction in any account that lays it to the side as a byproduct. This is just to say that even dissatisfaction may be a clue to what's most important about being human, and it may be a saving clue. Exploring this possibility will not be something that requires – nor can it have – certainty. That's a given. We live and act on faith. We choose on faith. We've not been given the option to do otherwise.

Faith. In this sense, the theist and the non-theist, the Catholic and the cold materialist, are in the same boat. Everyone is finally a person of faith to some extent. The only question is which faith we embrace in the course of our short lives.

So with this, we move another step closer to understanding the central work given to us as human beings. For many thoughtful people who have chosen materialism as a worldview, the goal is to clear away the illusory gloom of imperfection, sin and the sense of obligation to a non-existent entity so that life can be lived in its material fullness.

Likewise, the theist wants not an imposition of wishful thinking, stories or myths upon the world as it's lived, but rather to see the world as it is. The theist wants to know the truth about the mystery in the universe, the clue to our place in the universe. The theist believes that the ever-greater light into which God guides humanity is always, at the same time, an illumination of the object of guidance, which is created nature.

In the end, there are two kinds of thinkers. Those who say upon hearing the description of the many materially describable pieces and processes underlying the appearance, "This is all there is," and those who say, "No, it's not."

The former can say to the latter, "Show me why I should

accept the idea of something more," and though many arguments can be offered, offered indeed on both sides, one who starts as a materialist will attempt to account for these central experiences as purely material events, not yet explained, but explainable, while one who starts as a theist will say that these experiences are most fully illuminated when we reject the prospect that the determined material universe is all there is, and propose instead creator.

The theist will say that love makes more sense, truth makes more sense, value, morality, beauty, longing, joy, hope, music, mystery and goodness all make more sense in a universe that's not merely accidental matter. It's not an argument that such a thinker offers (although there are plenty of arguments) nor is it an argument that the materialist offers for the baseline and controlling belief that finally love, value, morality, beauty, longing, joy, hope, music, mystery, and goodness are temporary, accidental parts of a purely material universe.

Lived experience. At this deep level, it seems to me simply not to be about argument. It's about lived experience, experience lived as one aware, one awake, one compelled to ask questions and to understand. This is at the heart of what I take to be most important about being human. Among the awake who love, long, hope, value, create, and explore, some say matter is all there is, and from these lived experiences, accounts of great complexity can be elaborated. Others say there's more to the universe, and this view is also a threshold from which different accounts of great complexity can be elaborated.

But between the two at the fork is the human person, living a life, spending time, approaching death, and doing so without certainty, without a script, trying to know herself or himself, to know what's the case in the universe in which I, of all possible people, have shown up. Those like Pascal who do turn their attention to the truth of who they are in the shortness of their lives often find themselves frightened, and they find the contingency of their existence terrifying. "I'm terrified and surprised to find myself here rather than there, for there's no reason why I should be here rather than there, why now rather than then? Who put me here? On whose orders and whose decision have this place and time been allotted to me?"

Pascal notes that many are terrified by our blindness, by the silence of the universe where we're tucked off in some corner, lost without any clear reason for being here, no clear idea of what, if anything, we're supposed to do, like someone taken in his sleep to a terrifying, deserted island who wakes up with no knowledge of what's happened and no means of escape. In the middle of this overwhelming realization, Pascal looks around, and he sees others in the same situation.

But he notices that instead of despairing at this disorienting state of affairs, they've found some pleasant distractions and past times, and having become fond of these, they seem disinclined to further occupy themselves with these fundamental questions of who we are and what we ought to do. And in the face of this bewildering apathy, Pascal howls. "There must be more, and we should surely care about whether or not there is more, whatever the answer is."

Atoms in the void? When Pascal braces himself and opens his eyes, what does he find? The first thing he finds is that it's not enough to simply use words about the universe such as 'big' or 'vast.' He wants us to stretch our imaginations to the point of weariness in our attempts to grasp the dimensions of the universe. And even then, he says we must realize that we've not achieved true insight into our relative size.

So 400 years ago, he said, "The whole of the visible world is merely an imperceptible speck in nature's ample bosom. No idea comes near to it. It's an infinite sphere whose center is everywhere and whose circumference is nowhere." Such is space.

What if we go the other direction and consider ourselves, Pascal asks? We find yet another infinity, yet another abyss. As we move down to hand and to finger and to tissues and to organelles and to molecules and to atoms, Pascal wants us to lose ourselves in astonishment at their minute size. Holding our minds before an atom, he says, 400 years ago: "Let us see in it an infinity of universes, of which each has its own firmament, planets, and earth in the same proportion as in the visible world, in this land of animals, and ultimately, of mites in which we will find the same as in the first universe, and find again in others the same thing, endlessly and perpetually."

Turning this interrogation of limits of division towards our bodies reveals the dizzying height of our conscious experience of ourselves over the vast universe that is our body, comprehending such an incomprehensible number of parts. Thus is the conscious, experiencing unity called 'Me' caught between two infinities, one unthinkably large, and the other unthinkably small. We're practically nothing in compared to the size of the universe, and we're massive compared to the size of the single atom in our bodies.

PASCAL'S WAGER

QUESTIONS FOR DISCUSSION

What do you think is the central project or work of being human?

"Among the awake who love, long, hope, value, create, and explore, some say matter is all there is...Others say there's more to the universe." Which way does your view tend?

? For an audience question related to this topic (*Could you ever be convinced there is no God?*), see page 48.

WHAT IF THERE'S MORE?

But the question always returns for Pascal, "What if there's more?" What if your claim to being satisfied as a transient, though conscious vapor is merely the way in which you avoid recognizing that you would be incomparably more satisfied if God existed?

Pascal loves to use this language. He goes on and on for 500 pages, so you can imagine it's somewhat dreary. What if your experience of the universe as more than mere accidental matter were in fact a sense tethered to the truth? What if your longing, your love and your search for meaning could be met with something as ultimately satisfying as God?

Even to those who assert there is no God, and who say that we must find satisfaction elsewhere, Pascal wants to insist that if there *were* a God, that reality would make you happier, and if a God would make you happier in the truest sense, you are in some manner 'meant' for God, even as you're 'made' for water and find that it quenches your thirst, 'made' for bread and finds that it satisfies your hunger. In this phase of his argument, Pascal wishes primarily to shake us into honesty about what would constitute our deepest happiness.

Dissatisfaction as a clue. At this point Pascal is not trying to demonstrate anything about the truth of the universe, but rather to show us something about the truth of ourselves as human beings. Little can be said about what the truth of ourselves might suggest about the universe until we come clean with the acknowledgement that being atoms in the void is unsatisfying, that life as a conscious but transient, accidental vapor on a speck in the middle of an incomprehensibly massive universe doesn't fit what some of us experience as our deepest desire.

Now this is not a nurtured dissatisfaction that can be answered with a saint's response to modest goods, "Why can't you just be satisfied with your life?" Rather, it's an awareness of genuine and well-grounded dissatisfaction, and a refusal to make myself settle for less than what my inner urge is insisting ought to be the case. He wants us to seek truth with the same urgency a parent might seek for a child, thought to be lost forever, when some strange clue suggests things might be otherwise. A parent like that will never rest and will be thinking about the child even as they do other things in the day.

It is not, Pascal says, that we have to know what God is. If all were darkness with absolutely nothing suggesting the possibility that there's more – that there's a God – that would be easy. Or if all were light, with clear and absolute, unwavering signs of a creator God everywhere we look, that would be easy. But Pascal says that's not our state. We're awake, and we're aware, and we're certain to die. And instead of the desired certainty, Pascal says: "In the state in which I am, not knowing what I am or what I ought to do, I know neither my condition or my duty, but my whole heart longs to know where the true good lies in order to follow it." Only when someone is at that point are they ready to ask the important question in the face of our true condition as human beings: *What shall we do?*

Pascal is not in the business of proving God's existence, and people frequently get confused about this point. He is in the business of attending to probabilities – the stakes in a gamble – and the answer to the biggest gamble we have, namely, how we should live our lives.

The quest. Pascal wants to say that if it's even *possible* that there's more to the universe and myself than atoms in the void, and if it *might* be the case that this possible more is God, then it approaches *certainty* that I should include this in my life planning as I answer the question, *What should I do?*

This is as close as we get to certainty, according to Pascal. If there might be a God, my quest better include this possibility, or at least include some curiosity about the possibility. This is the starting point from which many of Pascal's own queries began, and he thinks the heart's convictions regarding love, meaning, longing, and so forth are sufficient to at least merit a hearing on the question whether there might be a God.

That said, he affirms scripture's characterization of God as a hidden God, and he thinks it's absurd to try to prove God's existence from what we encounter in the natural world. I don't go with him on that entirely. But many of us can affirm Pascal's experience of the universe from the perspective of faith, lighting up as a work of the God who is loved and served, illuminated with a kind of mystery and suggestiveness that has inspired much of the great poetry and art that even Nietzsche claimed could only be produced under the conviction that there's a God.

But Pascal wants to say if one looks at the world from the perspective of non-theism, there's little there that persuades one to believe. So he does not want to go in that direction. The organization of a grasshopper or the course of the moon inspires delight in someone who already believes in God, but he thinks if it's offered as a proof for the existence of God, however complicated the presentation, the argument inspires contempt. We're going to leave that to the side. I mentioned it because from his perspective, this is actually a good thing because it is at the point of deep uncertainty that he has something important to say.

QUESTIONS FOR DISCUSSION

If you're really honest, what would constitute your greatest happiness?

How do you respond to the idea that dissatisfaction can be a clue to the presence of something more? How do you typically respond to feelings of restlessness or longing?

How does curiosity about the possibility of God figure in your life planning?

PASCAL'S WAGER

Pascal wants to set things up as a gamble, and he wants to ask you, "So you want to gamble? All right, let's raise the stakes." Instead of trading on the value of a dollar or a poker chip, trade on the value of your life. This is not a trick. Pascal is claiming to have no more certainty about the existence of God than any agnostic or non-theist, at least for the purposes of articulating this starting point. Either there is a God or there's not. No matter how much you strain your reasoning abilities, he wants to say, you will not be able to prove with certainty the truth of the question, one way or the other.

But you are in the game, and you don't have a choice about whether you're in the game because here you are, alive, spending your time with no choice on whether you spend it. So consider the options. Suppose there's no God, and you've structured your life in accordance with this view as you ask, *What is it to be human?* When you're dead, there's nothing lost with this approach. While you were alive, you had some interesting ventures, ate some good meals, spent time with friends and enjoyed these things. Nothing lost.

Suppose on the other hand that there's no God, but you wager that there is a God, and you've structured your life according to this view. True, you will likely have spent time praying in an empty universe, will have joined a faith community, tried to follow what you take to be commands to love and to play fair, to not steal, to not kill, to not be promiscuous and so forth. You will have fostered habits of contemplation, and you will have probably read about a hope in a future life after death. You would have also had some interesting ventures, made some good meals, spent time with friends. You likely would have had some more rules attached to these activities following from your belief that God made you, and in order to flourish fully as a human being, you should use these gifts in accordance with guidance from the God who created you. But when you die, yet again, nothing is lost because you disappear. You turn into dust, and eventually the universe reverts to dead matter with no consciousness. So who cares? Ultimately, nothing is lost.

On the other hand, Pascal says, suppose that there is a God. But rather than wagering on this view, you structure your life as though there is no God. That life would be comparable to the woman sitting in the prison cell unaware of the good news that she's been exonerated and is free to leave the prison. It is, again, a life in which there are ventures, pleasures and risks. But it is a sad life because though there is an inexhaustible well of purpose and meaning in the universe, the meaning of everything we care about is experienced as though it's just a surprising and very temporary event in an otherwise non-conscious material universe.

It's living, Pascal says, in a universe where our longing for more actually can be met by God, but living as though that longing is nothing more than an illusion or something explained by our fears or habits, grounded like everything else in purposeless material events. That, Pascal wants to say with as much force as he can muster, is a far more unfortunate life than the life spent searching for God in a universe that has no God.

The final possibility, of course, is that we live in a universe created by God, and that despite our inability to fully understand God or even say what God is, nonetheless, our longing to *search* for God is inspired by the *existence* of God. And our search will not be in vain. And because only God can satisfy our longing for God, our hopeful search is our delight, since we're no longer pretending that something besides God can satisfy us.

Even if we experience doubt more than faith in the course

of our search, as almost certainly happens somewhere along the way, still we can affirm that human beings are creatures for whom only God is finally satisfying. We are in need of God, and in God alone is our deepest desire finally met. But in this universe, however faltering our way, we live as people of hope, and this hope will be answered.

So that's the wager. It is not a gimmick that's supposed to yield belief as though we could force belief. Rather, it's a way of acknowledging what's at stake as we look for the purpose of our lives, along with our unavoidable uncertainty and the urgency that's introduced by our mortality. Put another way, the end of a wager – both in the sense of its *goal*, but also in the sense of an argument coming to an end – is a challenge to live in a certain way.

Are you there? It's not an argument to feel a certain way. In one sense, the wager might be best thought of as a prayer that anyone can pray in honesty because it doesn't require specific belief, feeling, or any *a priori* conclusions, and the prayer is this: *Are you there?* The answer may be yes. The answer may be no. But here is the gamble that Pascal offers: the aspect of staking your life on the wager.

If the prayer is prayed well, it can't be prayed with a pre-set form the answer must take, nor with a timeline. For the answer may well not come in a form that can be expressed as a proposition or an argument, and this is what Pascal means when he says that the heart has reasons of its own that reason doesn't know. The answer is not necessarily a one-time *yes* or *no*, but may well be a process.

The habit of praying, *Are you there?* in the context of our various life activities is itself a habit of openness to the possibility of God. This habit of praying in this way can affect the character and capacity of the one wagering. The reason is that the very habit of approaching different parts of lived experience with a mere openness to the possibility of God may itself be a condition for seeing certain qualities in the world, certain parts of what's real about the world.

What if you are there? But there's a second question following from the first that can be used to probe the way value changes in the world. And the question is this: *What if you are there?* What difference would it make in this or that particular situation, for the answer to the question, *Are you there?* to be yes?

Now, it's fair to ask why we should bother with all this. The answer Pascal gives is that you will develop a habit of seeing one way or the other. The wager you're *forced* towards is to embrace a habit of looking at the world in a certain way, and as you do, it's reasonable to observe actively the consequences of the habit you have chosen as you encounter the world.

So for example, consider the encounter of a parent with her child whom she loves. In the face of uncertainty, we can develop the habit recommended by Bertrand Russell, which is to say that though we may call ourselves persons and see each other this way, we are in fact no more than physical mechanisms whose thoughts and bodily movements follow the same laws, "that describe the movements of stars and atoms."

For Russell, there's no distinction between persons and things, and what we call our thoughts seem to depend upon an organization of tracks in the brain in the same sort of way in which journeys depend upon roads and railways. The fact that roads and railways are deliberately placed by intention with a distinct purpose and goal is not likely an extension of the metaphor that Russell would approve.

So the parent sees her child and can say within worldview, "Fundamentally (fundamentally meaning at bottom), you're chemistry." And in so saying, she deepens the habit of seeing the world in a certain way. Now this is not a statement that's made in certainty. It's an understanding of the world as she has so far encountered it. It is one of several kinds of understandings she might have about the world that includes her child, chemistry and all.

Another kind of understanding can arise if the same parent, looking at her child, directs the beam of the second question that I derive from Pascal towards the situation. What if God is there? What if the answer to the first question – *Are you there?* – is yes? Does that in any way impact or change the meaning of the parent's response to her child? Does the child's apparent personhood and presence seem obscured, or does the truth seem clarified by the second question: *What if God is there?*

QUESTIONS FOR DISCUSSION

What are the options in Pascal's wager?

What are the risks of asking, "Are you there?"

Think of a recent experience of beauty or suffering that brought you lasting joy or pain. What if the answer to the first question – Are you there? – is yes? Does that in any way impact or change your response to the experience?

? For audience questions related to this topic, see page 39 (*Does Pascal's wager include an afterlife?*) and page 43 (*If you pray, couldn't you be deluding yourself in the answer?*).

PASCAL'S WAGER

LIVING OUT THE WAGER

Again, the purpose of the two questions is not to prove God's existence. Rather, it's a way of meaningfully living out the wager over the course of a life, and doing so with a corollary habit of observation and attention to the ways in which experience is illuminated. The wager is the way in which thinking and feeling people orient themselves towards the world as it's experienced.

Beauty. So we listen to music. Bach's concertos do not themselves compel us towards conclusions regarding their origin, meaning and purpose. But if we begin in a strict materialist universe with a kind of reductive naturalism, our starting point will lead us to devise theories and explanations that account for Bach's brain producing this music and our own brains hearing the music. Writing a concerto is just another interesting (interesting to us, at least) manifestation of determined chemical reactions that are, as chemical reactions go, qualitatively no different than a reaction in a beaker when a teaspoon of sugar dissolves in water (though the reactions in Bach's brain are more complex).

On the other hand, if we've wagered differently, we might, while listening to a Bach concerto, ask what the implications are if God is there. What's the effect of this alternate picture on our experience of music? Is there any way in which music makes more sense if there is a God? Is there any way in which it makes less sense?

Science. There's another kind of activity that is made interestingly complex in light of wagering one way or the other, and this is science. When, for example, we approach the meaning of data mined through evolutionary biology, will we do so like Francis Crick, who is an atheist, or like Simon Conway Morris, who is an evolutionary biologist at Cambridge University and a

Christian?

When we study the data and theory of physics and consider how this relates to the rest of our knowledge and experience, will we do so from the starting point of Stephen Hawking, who is sort of an atheist, or John Polkinghorne, who is a theoretical physicist and an Anglican priest? The data alone will not yield a worldview.

Suffering. Suffering and evil are likewise important aspects of our experience of wagering, and this in at least two ways, each of which is worthy of a much longer treatment than I can give here. First, we encounter the suffering and evil themselves. So children die of cancers in one decade, though they might have been saved in the next because of new medical discoveries. And the primary difference between the two decades is the advance of medical science. In the absence of God, that's not surprising. But is there any change in our experience of this suffering when in the middle of the experience we ask our two questions: *Are you there?* and *What if you're there?*

The first response that seems fitting, is that if you are there, why do you allow the suffering and loss to continue? And that's a kind of response that does contribute to uncertainty. But again, the wager Pascal wants to push us towards is not a propositional exercise we can do in our heads abstractly as though we're arguing points of utility. Rather, it's pulling us towards a lived life. To ask the questions from within the experience of suffering requires in some measure that you actually be in the middle of the suffering.

The wager is not a circumscribed arena for debate about why, if there is a God, thousands die in a tsunami in Japan. Rather, from within the lived experience of my suffering, the wager is lived. As I lay in my deathbed, struggling for breath, I pray, *Are you there? And what if you are there?* The rest is not really speakable because it can only be lived.

The wager does require an openness to answers that may surprise. A faith that has at its center the Son of God dying on the cross at the hands of the Roman army after asking God to let this cup pass, and crying out from the cross, "My God, my God, why have you forsaken me?" is not a faith that's likely to have simple, formulaic responses to our personal experience of suffering and prayerful lament.

So this is Pascal's wager. It's not that he desires the discomfort of our current state. Rather, it's that he sees the impossibility of our having it any other way. This doesn't mean living without joy. Far from it. It's actually an invitation in the face of uncertainty to live joyfully in the world, complete with all its beauty and all its suffering.

And that is my start to an answer of what it is to be human. And for my part, I would wish for anyone the joy I've had seeking after the truth in this world filled with beauty and suffering.

If you've ever hesitated to get on a roller coaster, worried over what's ahead, but finally sit in the seat and buckle yourself in, then you know the feeling that there's no way to do anything but ride the ride to the end. We are all most assuredly and irrevocably strapped in, and there's no way off the ride except to ride it to the end. But this very necessity itself can relieve our fretting. Wringing our hands will do no good.

So what is it to be human? I suggest that at least one answer is that being fully human is to love deeply, to wager boldly, and then to live fully. Thank you.

QUESTIONS FOR DISCUSSION

Try living out Pascal's wager for a week. What do you notice?

? For an audience question related to this topic (*As a pediatric oncologist, how does your philosophy affect your work?*), see page 49.

QUESTION AND ANSWER

PASCAL'S WAGER

Summary of Questions from the Audience

- Does Pascal's wager include the backdrop of an afterlife, of heaven and a hell? (Answer on page 39)

- If we found an intelligence that values love and truth, would it also be human? (Answer on page 41)

- If you ask the two questions (*Are you there? What if you are there?*) couldn't you be deluding yourself in the answer? (Answer on page 43)

- Is it possible to have a sense of meaning and feel significant, but actually have no meaning and be insignificant? (Answer on page 46)

- Could you ever be convinced that there is no God? (Answer on page 48)

- As a pediatric oncologist, how does your philosophy affect your work? (Answer on page 49)

- Do you see patients who are theists handle suffering differently or the same as materialists? (Answer on page 50)

- How do you relate meaning and purpose of our existence, and are they the same, or are they different, and how do you connect those to the self? (Answer on page 51)

Question and Answer Session

Audience member: In the past when I've heard Pascal's wager, it's always been against the backdrop of an afterlife, of heaven and hell. Is that accurate? Or is yours the real one?

Barfield: Mine is the argument that Pascal should have made. Pascal gives his argument in the *Pensées,* which is about 500 pages long, and he never turned it into a coherent piece of work. It's serial ideas. And many of them contradict each other. When you read through it, it can be quite a difficult process of trying to bring together a coherent thought and understanding what he is talking about. So one way of reading Pascal is most assuredly against a backdrop of eternal life, and he, in certain parts of *Pensées*, adds in the element of eternal risk.

And so for Pascal it is not just the idea that if there is a God and I choose to live my life as though there is no God, then I lose out on many wonderful, meaningful things in this life; he would add that my eternal destiny is also at stake. If there is no God and I live my life as if there is a God, and I come to an end and I turn to dust, all that happens is I turn to dust. But if I live my life as though there's no God and there is a God, then I may end up being damned for all eternity. And if I compare those two things, being damned for all eternity and turning to dust, well then I'm going to wager in the direction of least risk.

So that's a semi-crass way to summarize Pascal's argument. He's more nuanced, and I personally think that he's frequently misunderstood as trying to scare people into belief. I don't think that's what he's trying to do, and it's the reason I cast the argument in a slightly different form because I think that's what he's really trying to do. He is himself a Christian philosopher. And so in his own experience with God, he was convinced that if you will hurl yourself into this wager, risking openness to God, you will not find emptiness. You will start discovering things.

My take on Pascal is that he's primarily trying to prod us into seriously engaging with life and the possibility that there is a God.

Audience member: My question is going to be the nerdiest one tonight, I'm sure. But suppose we find a similar kind of intelligence either made by us or alien or whatever you want to call it, that values things like love and truth and hates things like injustice and suffering. In the context of tonight, is that just as human as we are?

Barfield: Well, if we find creatures like that, that's the discussion I'd like to have with them. When I think of creation, I think of creation as pervasive. For example, when I experience my dogs, Emma and Sophia, I experience genuine response from them that I find funny and interesting. I find that in their relationship to me, they do things that they might not if they weren't in a relationship to me. For example, they go outside to pee. They have a more complicated life in relationship to me. We have a sense of play, a sense of engagement, and I find that to be wonderful in light of what I take to be the created universe. I'm very grateful for this interaction with this animal.

Now if I found another creature that didn't share my same carbon-based makeup but was capable of love and joy and longing, then I would rejoice and would want to know what their experience of seeking after God is. I wouldn't require that that be human, necessarily. So I would be thrilled. Does that answer your question? I wouldn't require that they be human for them to love. Do you know what I'm saying?

Audience member: I could see it. I could find an answer in there.

Barfield: That's so generous.

Audience member: That you'll be happy about it is good enough for me.

Barfield: Well, I take it that your question is meant to say that if I'm going to insist that what's fundamental to being human is this sense of encountering beauty and suffering and all the other things I've used as place setters and responding to it in this genuine, urgent sense – if I'm taking that as central to being human as opposed to, say, being my dog or my cat – then if I find a non-human entity that engages in the same way, then this no longer can be reduced as sort of essentially human. Right?

Audience member: Yes, exactly.

Barfield: And so I think I would have to wait until I see one of those creatures, truly, to find out.

Audience member: Fair enough.

Barfield: If you see one, let me know.

Audience member: I want to make sure I'm understanding this right. Whenever you're talking about the two questions – *Are you there?* and *What if you are there?* – and you say develop an attitude of openness to those questions and to the existence of something, and make it a habit to ask those questions, does the searching for that weaken the validity when you find it? Because you're searching for it, is there a possibility of that being a human creation, a social construction?

Barfield: Uh-huh.

Audience member: Because you're looking for it.

Barfield: Yeah, sure. Of course that's possible. I mean that's part of the uncertainty – that's part of the risk that I'm talking about. And that's what I really think that Pascal and myself would want to argue for is – look, if there is a God, plunge in and see if you can find that God. You know?

Now if I'm going to worry over whether or not maybe I'm just deluding myself as I say, *Are you there?* then I'll never get started, especially if one of the requirements for seeing certain things is having an openness to this. So if I say, "Okay, I am absolutely not open to the possibility that God is there," then what I'll require is that I find God either in my laboratory experiments or with Hubble, or I'll find God some other way.

But if the condition is to actually have an open – and I'll use the word "prayerful" – response to our experiences of love and joy and so forth, if that's the condition for discovery, and you reject the condition for discovery *a priori*, well, it's going to be a lot harder to get there.

And it is a risk, absolutely. I mean it's like I said, if all was darkness: easy. If everything was pure light: easy. It's not. You're stuck. And so you have to decide how you're going to approach this sort of thing.

And the thing that I like about the question, *Are you there?* – and again, this is just me struggling in front of you guys – the thing I like about the question, *Are you there?* is that the many people who we take to be deepest in the things of God are people who are deeply involved in prayer, and they have said how important prayer is in the exploration of God.

To me, if someone makes a step towards claiming something about their belief or whatever, but it's not true, they're actually taking a step away from God because God is truth. And if I truly absolutely find myself without belief and I fake it, that's actually a step away from God as far as I'm concerned. So the question that I had for myself when I was thinking about this – and please feel free to disagree – the question I had is: if someone honestly looks at the world and finds themselves without any inkling, is there any sort of honest way that they can find their way into prayer if prayer were a condition for exploring God? And it struck me that even a materialist or a radical empiricist could say, "Well, if the condition for discovery is prayer, I don't see harm in asking, *Are you there?*"

Now that may be wrong. I don't know. When I talk with my friends who aren't theists, some go with that and some don't. But it just strikes me as the kind of prayer that has integrity for someone that is open to exploring the universe, but who does not yet believe in God. It doesn't seem to me to diminish their integrity if they say, "I don't believe there's a God, but you tell me that you believe and that prayer is the way to it, so I can at least pray this: *Are you there? Hey, are you there?*"

And the other question I think is also important. I'm going to do a thought experiment. I have love, joy, goodness, longing, beauty, music, children, persons, all these things. I'm just going to ask the question: So what if there was a God? Would this make more sense to me or less sense to me? And I'm going to do the same with suffering. If I'm in the middle of suffering, I'm going to do the same thing because this is not about generating, provoking or forcing myself to feel something. It's about finding the truth of things, and God wants us to find the truth of things.

Audience member: Earlier, you seemed to say that having a sense of meaning and feeling significant implies that there must be meaning and you must be significant. I'm worried that would be circular reasoning. Would you say that it's possible for us to have a sense of meaning and feel significant, but actually there not be meaning, and we actually are insignificant?

Barfield: Depends on what you mean because if the world is not created, if it really is just atoms in the void and that is all there is, then there's no purpose to the whole. I mean what purpose could there be. Right? Just – there it is. But the reason that I was arguing for the indisputability of meaning is even if that's the case, I guarantee you a lot of things mean a lot to me. Alexandra, my daughter, means something to me. My love for Micah, my son, is not a fact that I will allow dispute on. I absolutely value him. And when I teach him not to lie, I'm sensing that there is something I'm teaching him that is right and good, and it's a value that I truly value.

When my friends who aren't theists, who do think it's all an accident – when they love their children, they absolutely love their children. And so the presence of meaning is to me just not controversial.

The thing that is controversial to me is the second thing that I said: the meaning of meaning. So when I understand the meaning that I encounter in beauty, or the meaning I encounter in grappling with virtue, or the meaning that I encounter in my love for another person, or even the personhood of another person, the range of options available to me as a Christian for giving an account of that meaning is very different from the range of options available to someone who truly thinks the whole world is purposeless and accidental: "Wow, what a strange thing that we all mean something to each other. That's bizarre, that matter matters to itself. Completely strange." You know?

A friend of mine at Duke who is a philosopher named Owen Flannigan (used to be Catholic, is now an atheist) recently published a book called *The Really Hard Question: Meaning in a Material World*. And I want to say, "Owen, that *is* a hard question." And his boss, Alex Rosenberg, who is a cold materialist, says, "Owen, get over it. There's not any meaning." You cheat in his class, though, and he will take you to the principal's office because he values truth telling and that sort of thing.

So where the contradiction comes in is in the meaning of meaning. And I see more contradiction in trying to come up with an account for things as Alex Rosenberg does. There I see a lot of challenges in accounting for meaning. But that's part of the wrestle. Owen is in it. He's living his life, and he cannot let go of meaning, even though he's a strict materialist. He cannot let go of the possibility that things genuinely mean – they must mean – and he's trying to come up with an explanation for it. I just think mine is better.

PASCAL'S WAGER

Audience member: Could you ever be convinced that there is no God? Would it be even possible? Not that you necessarily foresee that it will ever happen. Because I feel as a strict empiricist, which I consider myself, I could be convinced that there is a God, even though I don't believe in one right now. But could you say the same for yourself? Could you ever be convinced that there's not one?

Barfield: Yeah, and it's not likely going to be by argument. We were talking earlier tonight about the fact there are a lot of great arguments on both sides. I'll tell you that I had an experience some years ago where not by argument but by grief in the presence of the suffering of a couple of children I was taking care of who died, I found myself really, really in darkness. And by darkness, I mean I felt the world – I felt meaning – empty. But not because of an argument. That was through experience.

And it was likewise through experience, through a continued openness that I had, that I continued exploring the truth of things. If there was no God, I wanted to know the truth. I'm not interested in perpetuating a comfortable myth. I have no interest in that at all. I am only interested in the truth of things.

And in the course of my life and experience, this is where I'm at. Now, being a theist, there are a lot of arguments that make a lot of sense to me that bolster my theism. Next semester, I'm teaching a class that some of the students at Duke asked me to teach on science, theology and the new atheism. And so we're going to go through Richard Dawkins, Richard Swinburne, Christopher Hitchens, David Bentley Hart, and we're going to do the back and forth, and it's going to be a lot of fun. It's going to be really interesting. But what we're interested in is the truth of things.

Audience member: As a pediatric oncologist, how does your philosophy affect your work? When you're dealing with kids and watching them suffer, how do you still find beauty and meaning, and how do you keep going, and how do you also encourage the families that are going through everything, too?

Barfield: Wow, that's a great question. Philosophy for me is not a discipline. It's not a department. It's an activity. It's an act. It's an act in which I most fully engage in the presence of suffering or in the presence of beauty. In a sense, you've got the history of philosophy, but then you've got a philosophical disposition, which is to be interested in the meaning of the event unfolding in front of you. So from that perspective, I can tell you that it was philosophy, this kind of openness, that led me to the darkness that we were just talking about.

And it was the philosophical act of continuing to be open and not merely stopping that led me to where I am right now. And so that's the role that philosophy plays. For me, it is just a persistent engagement with the meaning of the thing unfolding in front of me, and a persistent curiosity about what's occurring.

Now the pain part, that has taken practice. That has taken being with people and being undone and being remade. And just through experience, coming to learn how to be present to people who are suffering, and it's very difficult. It's the hardest thing about being in this field by far. It was far easier to learn the oncology than to learn how to sit by the bedside and not say anything.

PASCAL'S WAGER

Audience member: I had cancer when I was five years old and I hold your position as a theist. That position really helped my family get through it, and it added a new comfort. Do you see your patients who are theists handle suffering differently from those who are materialists?

Barfield: I see it complexly, and I'll tell you how. First of all, I see two things among theists who experience their child having cancer or dying. One is a sense of comfort that a sovereign God, even though I don't understand it, is in control. The other is acute, deep lament, pain like we were talking about. Christianity is not a stranger to pain, and at the heart of the heart of the heart of the story is Jesus saying, "My God, why have you forsaken me?" And I see plenty of that, too. That's part of what they engage in.

Interestingly, for my patients and their families who are not theists, there's not a terrible amount of surprise to the event. It's biology, and biology goes in directions that we don't want it to go. They say: "I'm devastated. I'm horribly sad. I'm going to miss my baby, but I mean it is what it is. We die. Sometimes we die early. Sometimes we die late. We die." And in some ways, there's a kind of stoic composure that I see in my patients who are not theists that I find very admirable. It's something that I've learned a great deal from.

So the response to suffering is much more nuanced than I knew before I went into this.

Audience member: How do you relate meaning and purpose of our existence, and are they the same? Or are they different? And how do you connect those to the self?

Barfield: I definitely think they're connected. When I personally think of purpose, I think of purpose in terms of the end towards which I'm moving. So I think in terms of human flourishing. And of course, because I'm a theist and because as a theist I view the universe as created, I view human flourishing as something that tends towards some end.

You can call that end whatever you want to. You know, Thomas Aquinas would describe it in terms of contemplation of God. But there are lots of ways that we could talk about what that end is.

When I think about purpose in terms of an end, meaning is something that I experience in a context that may in some ways relate to my end, but other times, may simply be the presence of something that I wonder at. I don't know how else to answer that. You can ask it again if you want. Maybe I can do better the second time.

Audience member: Is there something you could say or do that would prove both?

Barfield: That I'm not going to be able to do. Well, I could go back to page 1. I'm just kidding. It's a very important question, but I think one that's so deep and complex that I wouldn't know how to answer it in less than – well, we've got less than 30 seconds. It's a great question, though. All right, thank you.

QUESTIONS FOR DISCUSSION

PASCAL'S WAGER

From *Importance of the Question, Uncertainty of the Answer* **(page 3)**

- Professor Barfield admits it's easy to move from one distraction to the next, never asking the hard questions. So why are you taking the time to dig into the question of being human? What do you hope to gain from dwelling on this question?

From *What Sort of Universe Are We In?* **(page 7)**

- In the face of the vastness of universe and the complexity of our bodies, people have varied responses. How does the "infinity of universes" affect your thinking about your own significance?

From *Is It a Created or Non-Created World?* **(page 11)**

- Professor Barfield claims that the presence of meaning is indisputable. Do you agree?

- What does Professor Barfield mean by "the meaning of meaning"? How does meaning depend on whether you believe the universe is created or not?

- Professor Barfield emphasizes the importance of uncertainty in human experience. How does your uncertainty affect your ability to answer hard questions?

From *Why Are Things The Way They Are?* **(page 16)**

- What experiences of suffering have marked your life? How did (or do) those particular experiences fit with your view of the world as created or uncreated?

- How is your understanding or response to pain and injustice different if you start with love at the heart of the universe?

- Do you think of God more as an abstract concept or a relational being? Can you identify some experiences or people that have shaped this view?

From *Two Kinds of Thinkers* **(page 22)**

- What do you think is the central project or work of being human?

- "Among the awake who love, long, hope, value, create, and explore, some say matter is all there is…Others say there's more to the universe." Which way does your view tend?

From *What If There's More?* **(page 26)**

- If you're really honest, what would constitute your greatest happiness?

- How do you respond to the idea that dissatisfaction can be a clue to the presence of something more? How do you typically respond to feelings of restlessness or longing?

- How does curiosity about the possibility of God figure in your life planning?

From *Pascal's Wager* **(page 31)**

- What are the options in Pascal's wager?

- What are the risks of asking, *Are you there?*

- Think of a recent experience of beauty or suffering that brought you lasting joy or pain. What if the answer to the first question – *Are you there?* – is yes? Does that in any way impact or change your response to the experience?

From *Living Out the Wager* **(page 35)**

- If you're ready, try living out Pascal's wager for a week. What do you notice?

ABOUT THE VERITAS FORUM

The Veritas Forum hosts university events that engage students and faculty in discussions about life's hardest questions and the relevance of Jesus Christ to all of life.

Every year, hundreds of university community members host, plan and coordinate a Veritas Forum on their local campuses, with guidance from national and regional staff across North America and Europe.

We seek to inspire the shapers of tomorrow's culture to connect their hardest questions with the person and story of Jesus Christ.

For more information about The Veritas Forum, including recordings and upcoming events, visit www.veritas.org.

26986583R00038

Made in the USA
Lexington, KY
23 October 2013